Wilkinsburg
Middle School / Senior High
Library

Wilkinsburg
Middle School / Senior High
Library

NFL TODAY — THE STORY OF THE NEW ENGLAND PATRIOTS

NFL TODAY
THE STORY OF THE
NEW ENGLAND PATRIOTS

MICHAEL O'HEARN

CREATIVE EDUCATION

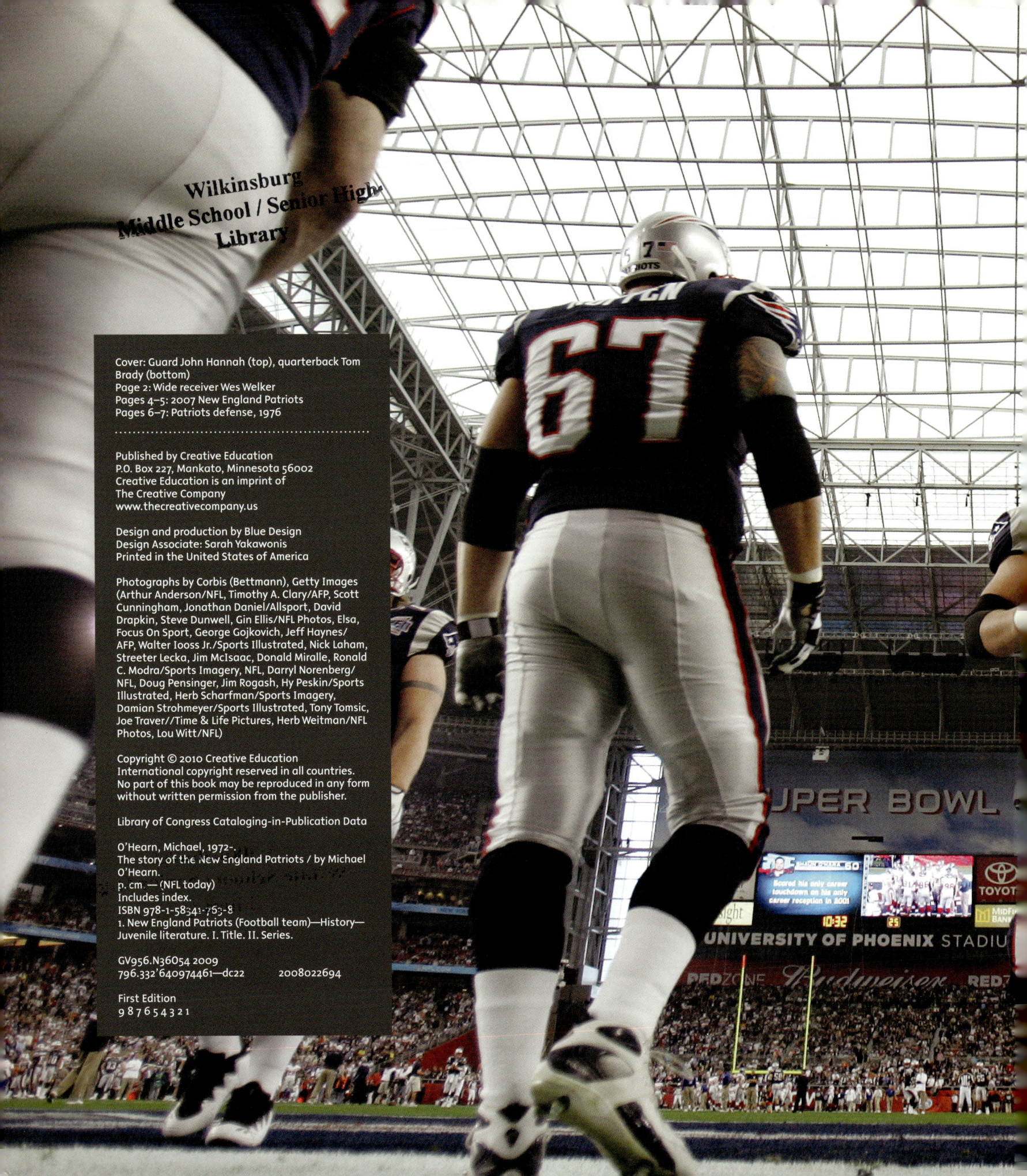

Cover: Guard John Hannah (top), quarterback Tom Brady (bottom)
Page 2: Wide receiver Wes Welker
Pages 4–5: 2007 New England Patriots
Pages 6–7: Patriots defense, 1976

Published by Creative Education
P.O. Box 227, Mankato, Minnesota 56002
Creative Education is an imprint of
The Creative Company
www.thecreativecompany.us

Design and production by Blue Design
Design Associate: Sarah Yakawonis
Printed in the United States of America

Photographs by Corbis (Bettmann), Getty Images (Arthur Anderson/NFL, Timothy A. Clary/AFP, Scott Cunningham, Jonathan Daniel/Allsport, David Drapkin, Steve Dunwell, Gin Ellis/NFL Photos, Elsa, Focus On Sport, George Gojkovich, Jeff Haynes/AFP, Walter Iooss Jr./Sports Illustrated, Nick Laham, Streeter Lecka, Jim McIsaac, Donald Miralle, Ronald C. Modra/Sports Imagery, NFL, Darryl Norenberg/NFL, Doug Pensinger, Jim Rogash, Hy Peskin/Sports Illustrated, Herb Scharfman/Sports Imagery, Damian Strohmeyer/Sports Illustrated, Tony Tomsic, Joe Traver//Time & Life Pictures, Herb Weitman/NFL Photos, Lou Witt/NFL)

Copyright © 2010 Creative Education
International copyright reserved in all countries.
No part of this book may be reproduced in any form without written permission from the publisher.

Library of Congress Cataloging-in-Publication Data

O'Hearn, Michael, 1972–.
The story of the New England Patriots / by Michael O'Hearn.
p. cm. — (NFL today)
Includes index.
ISBN 978-1-58341-759-8
1. New England Patriots (Football team)—History—Juvenile literature. I. Title. II. Series.

GV956.N36054 2009
796.332'640974461—dc22   2008022694

First Edition
9 8 7 6 5 4 3 2 1

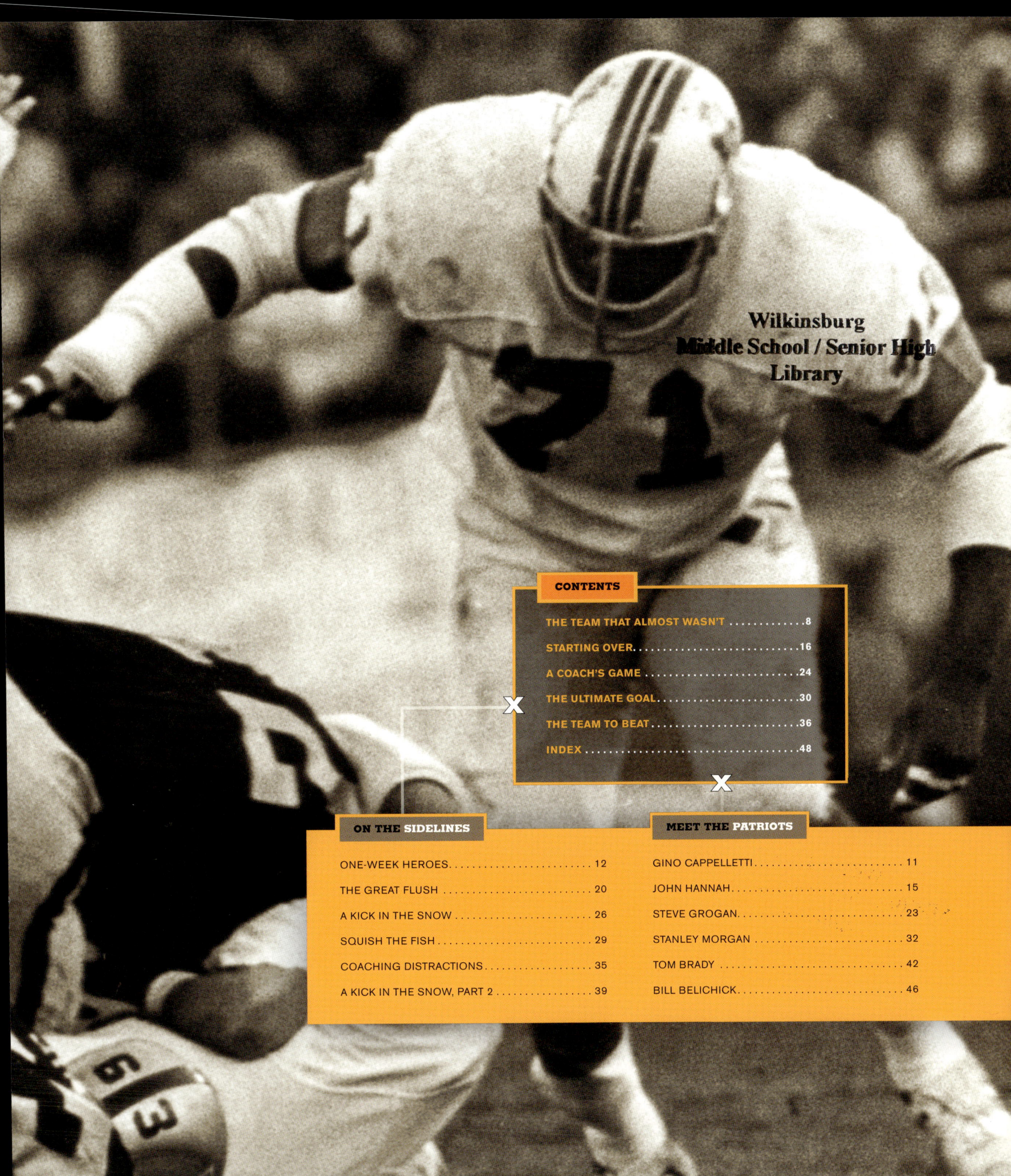

Wilkinsburg Middle School / Senior High Library

CONTENTS

THE TEAM THAT ALMOST WASN'T	8
STARTING OVER	16
A COACH'S GAME	24
THE ULTIMATE GOAL	30
THE TEAM TO BEAT	36
INDEX	48

ON THE SIDELINES

ONE-WEEK HEROES	12
THE GREAT FLUSH	20
A KICK IN THE SNOW	26
SQUISH THE FISH	29
COACHING DISTRACTIONS	35
A KICK IN THE SNOW, PART 2	39

MEET THE PATRIOTS

GINO CAPPELLETTI	11
JOHN HANNAH	15
STEVE GROGAN	23
STANLEY MORGAN	32
TOM BRADY	42
BILL BELICHICK	46

THE TEAM THAT ALMOST WASN'T

NFL TODAY: THE STORY OF THE NEW ENGLAND PATRIOTS

[8]

X The unofficial "capital of New England," Boston was steeped in sports tradition before the Patriots were born in 1960, home to such championship-winning teams as pro baseball's Red Sox.

America was born in New England. First settled by Pilgrims and Puritans seeking religious freedom, New England later led the struggle against English rule. The first battles of the American Revolution took place in Massachusetts at Lexington and Concord in 1775. Soldiers from Connecticut, Massachusetts, New Hampshire, Rhode Island, and Vermont all engaged in significant battles. These soldiers and leaders of the Revolution were called patriots. Men such as Samuel Adams, who led the Boston Tea Party, and Paul Revere, whose midnight ride warned of the British army's march to Lexington, were exciting figures, unflinching in the face of conflict and battle. It was therefore fitting that the region's football team was named the Patriots when it entered the American Football League (AFL) in 1960.

The Boston Patriots could also be called "The Team That Almost Wasn't." Founding owner Billy Sullivan had little money and no home stadium when he applied to join the new league, a rival to the established National Football League (NFL). Sullivan did have a gift for persuasion, however, and the AFL needed an eighth team. Boston, stadium or not, was an appealing choice. As New England's premier city, Boston remained the most populous city in America (and the largest television market) that did not yet have a professional football team.

After Lou Saban, a former NFL linebacker and college coach, was hired as the Patriots' first head coach, more than 350 players attended the team's training camp to try out. Ed "Butch" Songin won the quarterback job. Although he was 36 years old and had been out of professional football for 6 years, he would pass for more than 2,400 yards in 1960. Another training camp standout was Gino Cappelletti, who had been playing touch football to keep his skills sharp. A former college quarterback, he would make himself indispensable in Boston as both a kicker and wide receiver.

During the 1960s, the Patriots played their home games at Boston University Field, Boston College Alumni Field, Harvard Stadium, the Boston Red Sox's Fenway Park, and even Legion Field in Birmingham, Alabama. They finished a lowly 5–9 in 1960, and after opening the 1961 season 2–3, Saban was replaced by assistant coach Mike Holovak. On the field, Vito "Babe" Parilli, a former backup with the Oakland Raiders, took over as quarterback. Led by Parilli, the team turned the

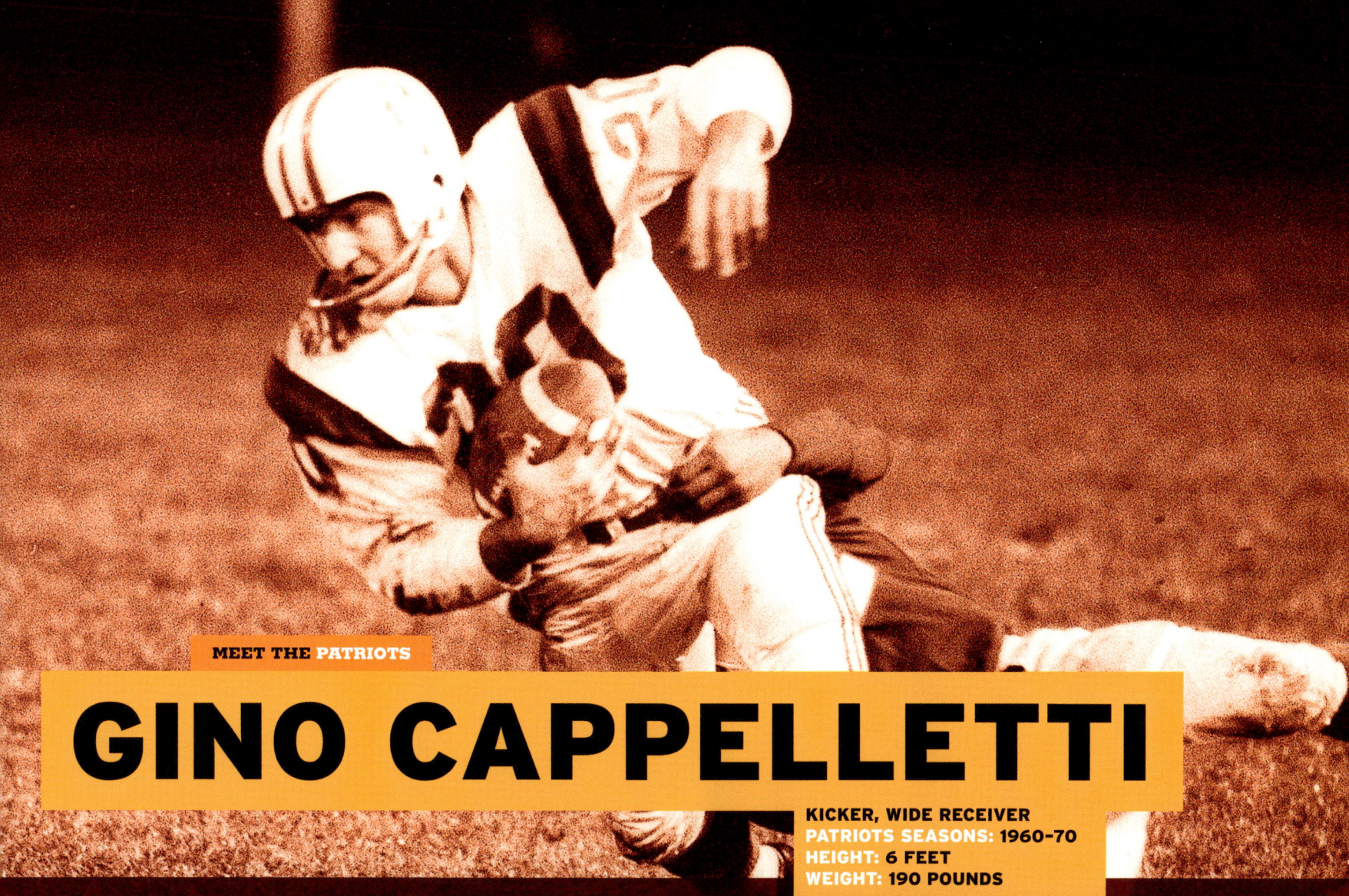

MEET THE PATRIOTS

GINO CAPPELLETTI

KICKER, WIDE RECEIVER
PATRIOTS SEASONS: 1960-70
HEIGHT: 6 FEET
WEIGHT: 190 POUNDS

Gino Cappelletti started playing college football in 1951 as a halfback for the University of Minnesota Golden Gophers. Unfortunately, the Gophers already had an All-American halfback, and Cappelletti realized he would remain on the sidelines unless he showed some versatility. So he switched to quarterback and proved his all-around skill by excelling at that position. After graduating, Cappelletti failed to make a pro team. When the chance came to try out for the Boston Patriots five years later, he was determined to earn a spot any way he could. He knew he didn't have the arm to play professional quarterback, but he had the leg to be a kicker. "Even as a kid, every team I was on, I wanted to be a kicker," he said. Still, he figured the team wouldn't sign a player who could only kick. He earned a roster spot as a defensive back, but during practice early in the 1961 season, Cappelletti found himself filling in at wide receiver. He caught a pass and never went back to defense. He played receiver and kicker his entire career, amassing an astounding 1,130 points.

ON THE SIDELINES
ONE-WEEK HEROES

Although the Boston Patriots' 1963 season was far from glorious, it offered the team its first taste of championship football. The Patriots opened the season a mere 2–3, and at the season's end, they were annihilated in the AFL Championship Game, 51–10, by the San Diego Chargers. But along the way, Boston won some key battles and captured the first playoff victory in team history. The unscheduled playoff was declared when Boston and the Buffalo Bills finished the season tied at 7–6–1. The two teams met in Buffalo in bitterly cold conditions on a slick, snow-covered field. Despite the weather, the Patriots attacked by air with long bombs and soaring kicks. Quarterback Vito Parilli hit running back Larry Garron with a 44-yard touchdown pass in the first quarter. In the third, he lofted a 51-yard completion to receiver Gino Cappelletti, which set up a 17-yard touchdown strike to Garron. As kicker, Cappelletti also chipped in four field goals and two extra points in the 26–8 Boston victory. For one week—until the unfortunate San Diego game—the Patriots were heroes.

season around to finish 9–4–1, good for second place in the AFL's Eastern Division.

The Patriots built a strong defense around the likes of linebacker Nick Buoniconti, end Bob Dee, and tackle Jim Lee "Hurricane" Hunt. Buoniconti was the inspirational leader of the group. Although many skeptics thought he was too small to play professional football, the 5-foot-11 Buoniconti used speed and smarts to become one of the greatest linebackers in pro football history.

The "Pats" held steady at 9–4–1 and second place in 1962 but dropped to 7–6–1 in 1963. Surprisingly, this record was strong enough to earn them their first postseason appearance, as the Patriots tied the divisional rival Buffalo

X In college, Nick Buoniconti (left) lined up not only at linebacker but at guard as well, learning to play low and with great leverage.

Bills. Boston defeated Buffalo in a playoff game but was then whipped 51–10 by the San Diego Chargers in the AFL Championship Game.

The Patriots came in second again in 1966, then finished with a losing record every season for the rest of the decade. Despite these lackluster results, players such as 240-pound, bulldozing fullback Jim Nance kept things exciting in Boston. "Guys would be bouncing off of him," Cappelletti recalled. Behind an offensive line anchored by seven-time All-Pro center Jon Morris, Nance piled up 5,323 career yards with the Patriots. Although a championship eluded the Patriots, by the end of the 1960s, The Team That Almost Wasn't had put down deep roots in New England.

Jim Nance rumbled for an average of 104 rushing yards per game in 1966, a Patriots record that has never been equaled.

MEET THE PATRIOTS

JOHN HANNAH

GUARD
PATRIOTS SEASONS: 1973–85
HEIGHT: 6-FOOT-2
WEIGHT: 265 POUNDS

Many people believe that John "Hog" Hannah was the greatest offensive lineman in the history of the NFL. A fierce competitor who hated losing, Hannah exploded off the line of scrimmage like a cannonball, and his ferocious blocks could change a game. "He'd be responsible for blocking a linebacker on a certain play, and before you knew it, the linebacker would be down, and without slowing down, John would be out ahead taking out a cornerback," said Patriots quarterback Steve Grogan. "He would get two or three guys on those sweeps like no one I've ever seen." Hannah worked hard to succeed and seemed to underestimate his own abilities. "Contrary to what people say, I'm not a natural athlete," he said. "I have some gifts, but I can't just go out there and do it. I've got to think about what I do, because if I don't practice well, I won't play well." Hannah was legendary for practicing at full-steam all the time, and it showed on the field. In 1991, he was inducted into the Pro Football Hall of Fame.

STARTING OVER

NFL TODAY: THE STORY OF THE NEW ENGLAND PATRIOTS

In 1970, the Patriots made a new start as the AFL merged with the NFL. For the Patriots, the merger posed challenges. For starters, the team still had no permanent home stadium, and its vagabond ways would not fly in the NFL. After various Boston stadium proposals failed, a plan to build in Foxborough, Massachusetts, succeeded, and construction on Schaefer Stadium began in 1970. The Patriots played to a dismal 2–12 record that year but improved to 6–8 in 1971, including an upset victory over the Raiders in Schaefer Stadium's inaugural game.

Because it was not based in Boston anymore, the team was renamed the New England Patriots. Rookie quarterback Jim Plunkett led the club's offensive attack with his strong arm, tossing 19 touchdown passes in 1971 and winning NFL Rookie of the Year honors. But neither Plunkett nor the new stadium turned the Patriots into a winning franchise. In 1973, Chuck Fairbanks, who had coached at the University of Oklahoma, was brought in to build a winner in New England.

Fairbanks's first move was to draft offensive lineman John "Hog" Hannah to give Plunkett better pass protection. Hannah also blocked for a running back who would become New England's all-time leading rusher: Sam "Bam"

X Even as their offense improved in the early 1970s, the Patriots consistently ranked near the bottom of the NFL defensively, surrendering 52 points in one 1972 game.

[17]

X One of the great bodyguards in the history of pro football, John Hannah protected quarterback Jim Plunkett for three seasons.

Cunningham. Cunningham was famed for his ability to leap over men piled at the line of scrimmage in short-yardage situations. Although he only once topped 1,000 yards in a year during his 9 Patriots seasons, he averaged an outstanding 3.9 yards per carry on 1,385 tries.

Their talent level was rising, but the Patriots never really jelled with Plunkett behind center. His best effort produced a middling 7–7 record in 1974. When Plunkett was injured in 1975, rookie quarterback Steve Grogan took over. That season

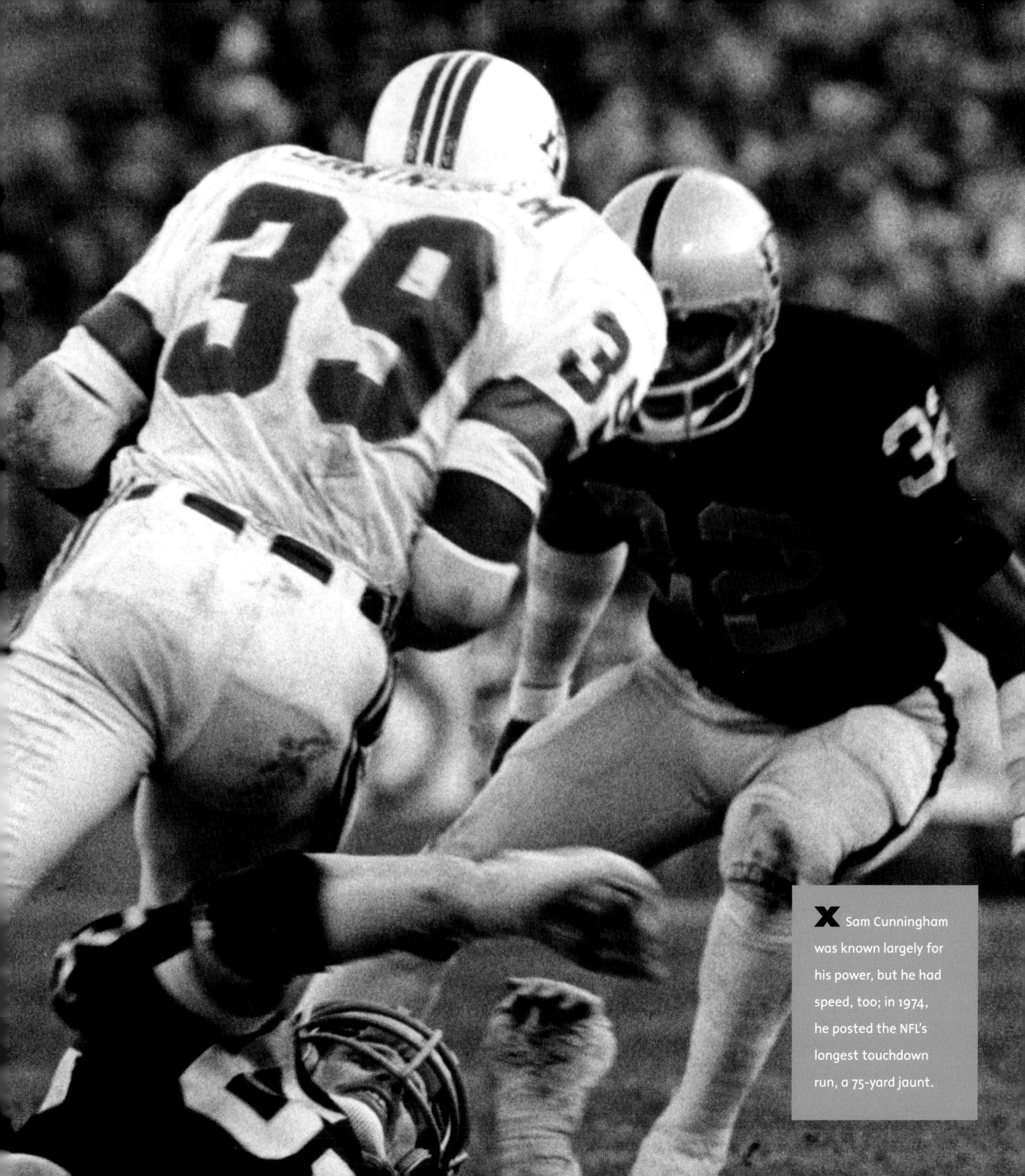

X Sam Cunningham was known largely for his power, but he had speed, too; in 1974, he posted the NFL's longest touchdown run, a 75-yard jaunt.

ON THE SIDELINES
THE GREAT FLUSH

The Great Flush was one of the most notable events of the Patriots' 1971 season. When 60,000 fans flooded the team's new Schaefer Stadium for an exhibition game against the New York Giants, they literally *flooded* the stadium. The toilets wouldn't flush, and the results were messy. Health inspectors threatened to take away the stadium's health permit, and without it, no games could be played there. So the Patriots made some fixes and set out to prove that the new plumbing could withstand 60,000 flushing fans. They enlisted staff, reporters, and anyone else they could find to execute The Great Flush. "It was funny," said Patriots announcer Gil Santos. "First we turned on every faucet in every sink. Then we started flushing like crazy." Sportswriter Ron Hobson partook in The Great Flush as well. "They had people all around at all the bathrooms," he explained. "And then when a horn blew, we all flushed at the same time. The feeling was if they could all work at the same time, that would be the supreme test. They did all work, and they got the permit."

turned out even worse at 3–11, but Grogan showed he could handle pressure. He also showed that he could scramble and pass as well as a younger Plunkett once had. Plunkett was soon traded, while Grogan led the 1976 Patriots to an 11–3 season and a playoff berth.

Wide receiver Darryl Stingley and tight end Russ Francis emerged as Grogan's favorite targets. Stingley was acrobatic and fearless in running routes across the dangerous middle part of the field, while the 6-foot-6 and 240-pound Francis possessed uncommon speed and soft hands for a player his size. On defense, cornerback Mike Haynes grabbed 8 interceptions and zigzagged his way to more than 600 yards returning punts in 1976. He would put his speed and instincts to work in seven stellar seasons with the Patriots en route to the Pro Football Hall of Fame. These players made New England a force to be reckoned with. "The '76 team was the best I ever played on," Hannah said.

The 1976 Patriots met the Raiders in the playoffs. New England had bested Oakland during the regular season and was playing with confidence when it arrived in Oakland. But confidence would not be enough. Oakland pulled out a 24–21 victory when quarterback Ken Stabler ran in a touchdown with 10 seconds remaining.

After a 9–5 season in 1977, New England came back strong in 1978, winning the American Football Conference (AFC) East Division and reaching the playoffs again. But it was a bittersweet year that ended badly and started even worse. Going for a catch in a preseason game against Oakland, Stingley took a vicious hit that left him paralyzed. The team rallied in the face of Stingley's sad and unexpected exit, earning 11 wins. It could not, however, rally in the playoffs. Foxborough's first-ever playoff game saw the Patriots get pummeled by the Houston Oilers, 31–14. New England would have to wait for another shot at the big game.

Andy Johnson (left) and Sam Cunningham (right) gave the Patriots a balanced one-two rushing punch in 1978, combining for 1,443 yards and 11 touchdowns.

NFL TODAY: THE STORY OF THE NEW ENGLAND PATRIOTS

MEET THE PATRIOTS

STEVE GROGAN

QUARTERBACK
PATRIOTS SEASONS: 1975-90
HEIGHT: 6-FOOT-4
WEIGHT: 210 POUNDS

Steve Grogan was a tough quarterback. During his career, he endured knee surgeries, elbow surgery, neck surgery, broken bones, separated shoulders, damaged ligaments, and several concussions. But if it was physically possible, he played. Grogan loved the rough-and-tumble game. Patriots center Bill Lenkaitis said this was never more obvious than when Grogan threw an interception. "Most quarterbacks try to hide," he said. "Grogan ran down and tried to knock the guy's head off." But Grogan wasn't all brawn and guts. He also had serious skill. He passed with precision for nearly 27,000 career yards, often tossing long bombs to his speedy receiving corps. The lanky field general also kept opposing defenses off-balance with his scrambling and running ability. In 1976, he rushed for 12 touchdowns, the NFL's single-season record for quarterbacks. Grogan's hard-nosed style of play often landed him at the doctor's office, but it also earned his teammates' respect. As Hall of Fame offensive lineman John Hannah said, "He was the kind of guy you wanted to protect, the kind of guy you wanted to play for."

A COACH'S GAME

Perhaps more than any other sport, football is a coach's game, with outcomes decided by strategy, game-time decisions, and the ability to manage and motivate players. After the departure of Chuck Fairbanks in 1978, the Patriots' success diminished according to the ability of their coaches.

Coach Ron Erhardt was too easygoing. His teams started strong but finished poorly, dropping five of their last eight games in 1979, five of their last nine in 1980, and their last nine en route to a 2–14 record in 1981. Erhardt failed to control his players, while his successor, Ron Meyer, tried too hard to control them. Meyer made unnecessary rules, such as no sitting on helmets during practice and no popsicles at training camp. While he earned better results—a 5–4 record in 1982 and an 8–8 mark in 1983—than Erhardt had, his players rebelled against him, and he was fired halfway through his third season.

Former Patriots assistant coach Raymond Berry had been away from football for two and a half years when the team

Players such as longtime linebacker Johnny Rembert turned the Patriots defense into a force in the early '80s, even as New England struggled to find the right head coach.

ON THE SIDELINES

A KICK IN THE SNOW

On a freezing December afternoon in 1982, the Patriots met the Miami Dolphins on an ice- and snow-covered Schaefer Stadium field. Linemen had little traction for blocking. Running backs slipped and slid. Kickers found no footing to launch their kicks. In the second quarter, Patriots kicker John Smith missed an 18-yard field goal. "My leg went flying up in the air, and I drove the ball right into John Hannah's butt," he said. Dolphins kicker Uwe Von Schamann muffed a 45-yarder—also into a lineman's backside. The game remained scoreless until New England gained a final chance with under five minutes remaining. That's when Patriots coach Ron Meyer called a play for Mark Henderson, driver of the tractor and snow sweeper used to clear the yard lines. "We had called timeout so John Smith could clear a patch for himself. Then I saw the sweeper and just went down and told him to sweep," Meyer said. "Great coaching genius, I guess." Henderson cleared Smith a spot from which to kick, and Smith knocked one through the uprights for a 3–0 New England victory.

[26]

offered him the head coaching job in 1984. A kind man who was well liked, Berry encouraged his team with a respectful coaching style. "He treated everyone like a man," Patriots linebacker Steve Nelson said. "He assumed we had the same goals he had—to win every game."

Nelson, who spent his entire 14-year NFL career with New England, was one of the leaders on Coach Berry's team. He met opposing ballcarriers like a brick wall, collecting more than 100 tackles in 9 different seasons. If Nelson was a wall, Andre Tippett was a hurricane. One of a new breed of outside linebackers that emerged during the 1980s, Tippett was fast and brutal. He could chase down smaller running backs and was just as effective at storming the passer. Tippett recorded 16.5 sacks in 1985 and would eventually set the Patriots' career mark of 100 sacks. Opposing offenses who tried to throw over the Patriots' ferocious linebackers had to contend with star defensive back Raymond Clayborn.

The Patriots got off to a slow 2–3 start in 1985 but then rattled off six straight wins after Steve Grogan took over for an injured Tony Eason at quarterback. When Grogan was injured late in the season, Eason returned and won three of four games to lead New England into the playoffs with an 11–5 record. Speedy wide receiver Stanley Morgan was a favorite target of both passers. The Patriots' true offensive strength, however, was their dominant running game, which was led by halfback Craig James and piled up more than 2,300 yards. Veteran guard John Hannah played heroically through numerous injuries to anchor the offensive line in his final season.

In the playoffs, New England won three road games, including a comeback from 17–7 down against the Los Angeles Raiders and a 31–14 rout of the Miami Dolphins in the AFC Championship Game. In the Super Bowl, however, New England was flattened by the mighty Chicago Bears, 46–10. To the puzzlement of many fans and even players, the Patriots came out passing despite having relied on their running game all year. "Well, the one thing the Bears can't say today is they stopped our running game," said James. "Because we didn't run it."

New England went 11–5 again in 1986 but lost to the Denver Broncos in the first round of the playoffs. The team fell to 5–11 by 1989, Berry's last year, and hit rock bottom at 1–15 the next year under new coach Rod Rust. The Patriots were down again.

ON THE SIDELINES
SQUISH THE FISH

When the Patriots faced off against the Miami Dolphins in the 1985 AFC Championship Game, they had something to prove. They had not won a game in Miami's Orange Bowl stadium in 19 years. But fresh off two road playoff wins, New England's players seemed unconcerned with the past and took advantage of soggy field conditions with a punishing ground game. "[The coaches] came to the offensive line and said, 'It's on you,'" said Patriots center Pete Brock. "'Oh, boy,' we thought, 'we're gonna run the ball in the mud.' And we did." The Patriots amassed 255 yards on 59 carries, with halfback Craig James rushing for 105 yards behind the muddy offensive line. The Patriots also recovered four Miami fumbles en route to a 31–14 victory. "It was 'Squish the Fish,'" said Patriots linebacker Andre Tippett. "We had never won down there, but we just walked into the Orange Bowl, and we weren't going to be denied." With the team's first victory in the Orange Bowl, New England also reached its first Super Bowl.

THE ULTIMATE GOAL

> The Patriots aired the ball out like few teams in the NFL in the mid-1990s; in 1994, 1995, and 1996, young quarterback Drew Bledsoe led the league in pass attempts every year.

After their abysmal 1990 season, the Patriots needed dramatic change. They got it in the form of new ownership in 1992 and a new coach and new look in 1993. Out was the team's old-fashioned, colonial-garbed hiking patriot logo, and in was a modern, grim-faced logo. Also in was coach Bill Parcells, who had won two Super Bowls at the helm of the New York Giants. When team ownership changed hands yet again in 1994, local businessman Robert Kraft provided the leadership necessary to build a championship team.

The new-look Patriots' first move was to select quarterback Drew Bledsoe with the first overall pick of the 1993 NFL Draft. In just his second season, Bledsoe led New England to a seven-game winning streak and its first playoff appearance since 1986. But the 10–6 Patriots lost to the Cleveland Browns in a muddy first-round game in Cleveland Stadium, with Bledsoe throwing three interceptions. "Right now," Bledsoe said, "it feels like a disaster, because we just lost. But I guess if you look at it with some perspective, it was a good season."

In 1995, Bledsoe injured his shoulder, and New England dipped to 6–10. One bright spot, however, was the play of rookie running back Curtis Martin, who cut and slashed his way to 1,487 yards and 14 touchdowns. Martin, Bledsoe, and

MEET THE PATRIOTS

STANLEY MORGAN

WIDE RECEIVER
PATRIOTS SEASONS: 1977–89
HEIGHT: 5-FOOT-11
WEIGHT: 181 POUNDS

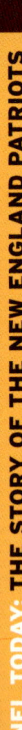

NFL TODAY: THE STORY OF THE NEW ENGLAND PATRIOTS

Stanley Morgan, wrote one reporter, was a "touchdown waiting to happen." His quickness and straight-ahead speed allowed him to average 19.4 yards per reception in an era when defensive backs were permitted to bang receivers all the way down the field. Morgan had a knack for keeping defenders on their heels and then leaving them in the dust. "When he was running those posts, those free safeties had to really get on their horse and get back there because he'd get on top of you in a hurry," Patriots coach Bill Belichick said. And once he caught the ball, Morgan was off to the races, with the end zone as the finish line. He was one of the game's speeding bullets, often gone before defenders could get a hand on him. "I remember Stanley going deep on those go-routes with nobody out there to catch him," said Patriots linebacker Andre Tippett. "Whenever you saw him open like that, you knew it was a touchdown." In 1989, Morgan caught his 67th Patriots touchdown reception, which remains the most in team history.

their teammates rebounded big time in 1996. The offensive line, anchored by tackle Bruce Armstrong, kept Bledsoe healthy, and wide receiver Terry Glenn proved a long-ball threat, setting an NFL rookie receiving record with 90 catches. Adding more muscle to the Patriots' air attack was Ben Coates, a big, powerful, and fast tight end. "We have as many weapons as probably anybody in the league right now," Bledsoe said.

Loaded with talent, the 1996 Patriots went 11–5 and made the playoffs. They trounced the Pittsburgh Steelers in a foggy game in Foxborough and dispatched the Jacksonville

X A six-time Pro-Bowler, tackle Bruce Armstrong (right) was widely regarded as the second-best offensive lineman in team history, after John Hannah.

Jaguars in a bitterly cold AFC Championship Game the following Sunday. Led by defensive end Willie McGinest, linebacker Chris Slade, and safety Lawyer Milloy, the Patriots' dominating defense held their opponents to nine points and no touchdowns over the course of the two playoff games.

In Super Bowl XXXI, the Patriots trailed the Green Bay Packers for much of the game but refused to fade. They came back from a 10–0 deficit in the first quarter to take a 14–10 lead and climbed to within striking distance at 27–21 after being down 27–14 at halftime. In the end, though, Green Bay's strong offense and stellar kick-return play proved to be more than New England could overcome in a 35–21 loss.

Coach Parcells left the team after the loss, and the Pats steadily sank. In 1997, they won one game fewer than in 1996 and lost in the second round of the playoffs. In 1998, they won one game fewer than in 1997 and lost in the first round of the playoffs. And in 1999, they won one game fewer than in 1998, leaving them at 8–8 and out of the playoffs. Once more, it was time for a change.

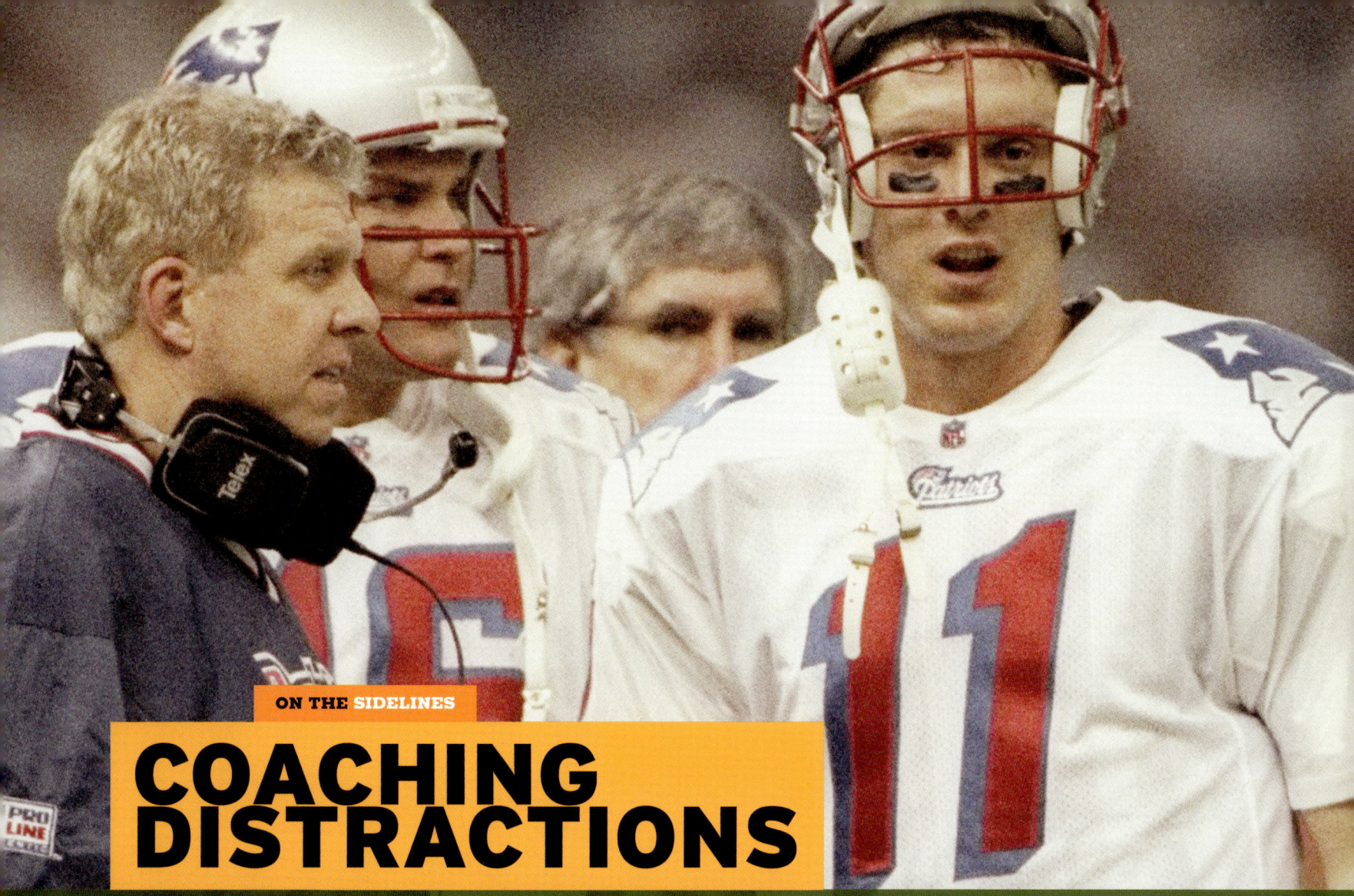

ON THE SIDELINES
COACHING DISTRACTIONS

It felt like déjà vu. Bad luck struck the Patriots heading into big games nearly 20 years apart. In 1978, before the season's final game, news leaked that coach Chuck Fairbanks was quitting to take a job with the University of Colorado. Fairbanks and owner Billy Sullivan bickered publicly while the team prepared to enter the postseason. "It took anything we had out of us for the playoffs," cornerback Raymond Clayborn said. New England was soon walloped by the Houston Oilers in the first round of the playoffs. The same drama repeated itself as the 1996 Patriots prepared for Super Bowl XXXI. News surfaced that coach Bill Parcells (pictured) would quit after the season. Although Parcells and owner Robert Kraft handled the situation better than their predecessors, the rumor was still a distraction, as news stories and media questions focused on Parcells's plans as much as on the game itself. "When we went to the Super Bowl, it was turned into a deal where it was Bill Parcells versus the Green Bay Packers," Patriots quarterback Drew Bledsoe later said. As was the case in 1978, the 1996 Patriots came up short on the scoreboard.

THE TEAM TO BEAT

NFL TODAY: THE STORY OF THE NEW ENGLAND PATRIOTS

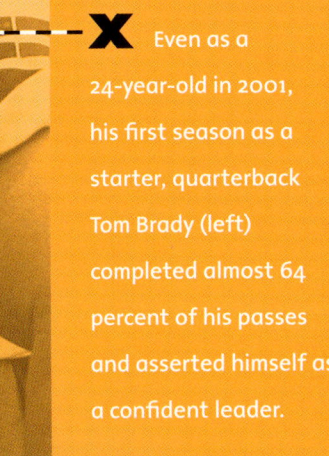 ✗ Even as a 24-year-old in 2001, his first season as a starter, quarterback Tom Brady (left) completed almost 64 percent of his passes and asserted himself as a confident leader.

When Bill Belichick led New England to a 5–11 record in 2000, his first season as the Patriots' new head coach, many fans thought Belichick's hiring had been a mistake. Although he had proven himself a brilliant defensive coordinator, engineering the dominating New York Giants defense of the 1980s, he had been unsuccessful in five years as the Cleveland Browns' head coach. But Belichick, along with owner Robert Kraft, had a plan to build a winner: assemble a group of team players that could achieve more than the sum of its stars.

A key piece of this plan fell into place in the second game of the 2001 season, when second-year quarterback Tom Brady stepped in for an injured Bledsoe. The Patriots lost that game, and for the next eight contests, Brady's play was spotty. But Belichick saw something in Brady. It wasn't pure physical ability. It was his intangible skills. Brady was a natural leader.

Belichick stuck with Brady, even after Bledsoe recovered, and the coach's faith in the young quarterback paid off. In the 11th game of the season, a victory over the New Orleans Saints, New England jelled as a unit. It didn't lose another game the rest of the year, including Super Bowl XXXVI, in which the Patriots shocked the highflying and heavily favored

St. Louis Rams, 20–17, on a last-second field goal by kicker Adam Vinatieri. "You can't beat a team like the Rams with individuals," Lawyer Milloy said. "It takes a team. That's what you saw today."

The championship-clinching upset was a true team effort. While Brady won the game's Most Valuable Player (MVP) award, Vinatieri could also have taken that prize. Or it could have gone to linebacker Tedy Bruschi or other players on the Patriots defense, which held the Rams to 17 points—14 below their season average.

Teamwork and smart play kept the Patriots rolling in the seasons that followed. In 2003, New England went 14–2 to win the AFC East. In the playoffs, New England first faced a tough Tennessee Titans squad and prevailed, 17–14. Then, in the AFC Championship Game, New England battled the Indianapolis Colts, who were emerging as archrivals. The Patriots' physical defense stifled the Colts' potent offense, creating five turnovers in a 24–14 victory. Super Bowl XXXVIII, between the Patriots and the Carolina Panthers, again came down to the wire. In the fourth quarter, with the score tied 29–29, Brady led his team down the field to set up a 41-yard field goal try by Vinatieri with four seconds remaining. Once again, Vinatieri sealed the victory.

ON THE SIDELINES

A KICK IN THE SNOW, PART 2

The snow was swirling, the wind was whipping, and the game was on the line. But like the New England winter itself, Patriots kicker Adam Vinatieri had ice in his veins. It was January 19, 2002, and the Patriots trailed the Oakland Raiders 10–13 in an AFC playoff matchup. With 27 seconds left in the game, 4 inches of snow on the ground, and 45 yards between him and the goalposts, Vinatieri stepped onto the field. He knew he had to make the kick or the season was over. Raiders coach Jon Gruden called a timeout, trying to "ice" the kicker by giving him time to grow nervous. "I'm not sure 'icing the kicker' actually works," Vinatieri said. "I think having a little extra time to clear the footing helps the situation." Despite Gruden's ploy, the snowy conditions, and the nerve-racking circumstances, Vinatieri knocked a low, warbling kick through the uprights. "I don't know if I've ever kicked in conditions worse than that," Vinatieri said. "It's probably the biggest kick I've ever had." For good measure, Vinatieri also booted a 23-yard game-winner in overtime.

X Versatile halfback Kevin Faulk was a valuable offensive weapon in the Patriots' wins in Super Bowls XXXVI, XXXVIII, and XXXIX.

MEET THE PATRIOTS

TOM BRADY

QUARTERBACK
PATRIOTS SEASONS: 2000–PRESENT
HEIGHT: 6-FOOT-4
WEIGHT: 225 POUNDS

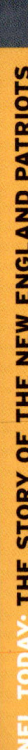
NFL TODAY: THE STORY OF THE NEW ENGLAND PATRIOTS

In 2001, Tom Brady's first season as the Patriots' starting quarterback, the team won its first Super Bowl. By 2008, they had won two more. One could argue that he owed his success to his hard work in practice, his preparation, and his determination to always improve—and all of these things would be true. But at the heart of it, Brady won because he played his best when it counted the most. "Nerves come from not knowing what to do," Brady explained. "If you're confident going out there that you know what you're going to do … that's when you feel best." Not particularly fast or strong-armed, Brady overcame any physical shortcomings with his poise and intelligence. "He can see the defense, what they're doing, and can sort it out in a hurry," Lloyd Carr, Brady's college coach at the University of Michigan, said of his former star. "You'll never see him panic." While Brady earned a reputation as one of the greatest quarterbacks of all time, he also became something of a style icon off the field. In 2007, *Esquire* magazine called him the "best dressed man in the world."

The next year, the Patriots again went 14–2. They crushed the Colts 20–3 in the playoffs behind running back Corey Dillon's 144 rushing yards, then triumphed over the Steelers in a 41–27 AFC Championship Game slugfest. In a Super Bowl matchup against the Philadelphia Eagles, wide receiver Deion Branch tied a Super Bowl record by grabbing 11 receptions, and the Patriots' defense held off a late Eagles charge to preserve a 24–21 victory.

The Patriots came down to earth with playoff losses in 2005 and 2006. Then, in 2007, New England came within one game of football immortality. After adding new star receivers in Randy Moss and Wes Welker, the Patriots went undefeated in the regular season, setting a new NFL scoring record with 589 total points. After beating the Jaguars and San Diego Chargers in the playoffs, New England reached its fourth

> ✕ Adam Vinatieri's clutch Super Bowl field goals had some football historians calling him the greatest kicker of all time.

X A 6-foot-6 and 310-pound giant, end Richard Seymour was a perennial Pro Bowl pick and the leader of the Patriots' attacking defensive line.

Super Bowl in seven years and stood poised to become the first 19–0 team in NFL history.

The heavily favored Patriots met the New York Giants in Super Bowl XLII and seemed to have the game in hand when they took a 14–10 lead with under three minutes remaining. But the Giants mounted an 83-yard drive, scoring a touchdown with 35 seconds left to upset the nearly perfect Patriots 17–14. "I think we all feel the same way," Belichick said. "I wish we could have done one thing a little better, and it might have changed it. But we didn't."

X Randy Moss set an NFL record with 23 touchdown receptions in 2007, then caught another in Super Bowl XLII versus the Giants.

MEET THE PATRIOTS

BILL BELICHICK

COACH
PATRIOTS SEASONS:
2000–PRESENT

NFL TODAY: THE STORY OF THE NEW ENGLAND PATRIOTS

Bill Belichick learned his Xs and Os at an early age from his father Steve, a former NFL player and longtime head coach at the U.S. Naval Academy. Belichick played high school and college football, and he began his NFL coaching career with the Baltimore Colts in 1975 at age 22. As of 2008, Belichick had more years of NFL coaching experience than any other active head coach. And as the Patriots' head coach, he achieved success by keeping his focus on football and on each game ahead. It never seemed to matter if key players were out of the lineup, what the media was talking about, or what the weather was going to be—Belichick stayed focused on the game. "You just try to take the situation at hand and do the best you can with it," he said. "When it is over, recalibrate, reload, and go again." Although his reputation took a hit in 2007 when it was revealed that he authorized the secret, illegal videotaping of opposing teams' coaching signals, he was widely regarded as one of the greatest strategists in the game.

 Despite the Patriots' bitter Super Bowl loss to the Giants, players such as linebacker Adalius Thomas promised to keep them in title contention.

In 2008, New England's title hopes seemed to go up in smoke in the very first game, when Brady was lost for the year with a knee injury. But backup quarterback Matt Cassel would not let the season go to waste, stepping into the starting role and throwing 21 touchdown passes to nearly lead the Patriots to another division title with an 11–5 mark.

New England has come a long way since its humble, homeless beginnings almost 50 years ago. After enduring some tough times in the 1960s and '70s, and then finishing as Super Bowl runners-up in the '80s and '90s, the Patriots became an NFL dynasty in the new century, hoisting the Lombardi Trophy three times in four appearances in the big game. Representing the proud New England region, today's Patriots plan to fight their way to more championships in the seasons ahead.

INDEX

AFC Championship Game 28, 29, 34, 38, 43
AFL Championship Game 12, 14
AFL seasons 9–10, 13–14
AFL-NFL merger 17
Armstrong, Bruce 33
Belichick, Bill 32, 37, 45, 46
Berry, Raymond 24, 27, 28
Bledsoe, Drew 31, 33, 35, 37
Brady, Tom 37, 38, 42, 47
Branch, Deion 43
Brock, Pete 29
Bruschi, Tedy 38
Buoniconti, Nick 13
Cappelletti, Gino 10, 11, 12, 14
Cassel, Matt 47
Clayborn, Raymond 27, 35
Coates, Ben 33
Cunningham, Sam 17–18
Dee, Bob 13
Dillon, Corey 43
division championships 22, 38
Eason, Tony 27
Erhardt, Ron 24
Fairbanks, Chuck 17, 24, 35
first season 10
Francis, Russ 21
Garron, Larry 12
Glenn, Terry 33
Grogan, Steve 15, 18, 21, 23, 27
Hannah, John 15, 17, 21, 23, 26, 28
Haynes, Mike 21
Holovak, Mike 10
Hunt, Jim Lee 13
James, Craig 28, 29
Kraft, Robert 31, 35, 37
Lenkaitis, Bill 23
Martin, Curtis 31
McGinest, Willie 34
Meyer, Ron 24, 26
Milloy, Lawyer 34, 38
Morgan, Stanley 27, 32
Morris, Jon 14
Moss, Randy 43
MVP award 38
Nance, Jim 14
Nelson, Steve 27
NFL records 23, 33, 43
Parcells, Bill 31, 34, 35
Parilli, Vito 10, 12
Patriots name 9, 17
perfect regular-season record 43
playoffs 12, 14, 21, 22, 27, 28, 29, 31, 33–34, 35, 38, 39, 43
Plunkett, Jim 17, 18, 21
Pro Football Hall of Fame 15, 21
Rookie of the Year award 17
Rust, Rod 28
Saban, Lou 10
Schaefer Stadium 17, 20, 26
Slade, Chris 34
Smith, John 26
Songin, Ed 10
Stingley, Darryl 21, 22
Sullivan, Billy 9, 35
Super Bowl 28, 29, 34, 35, 37–38, 42, 43, 45, 47
Super Bowl record 43
team records 27, 32
temporary stadiums 10
Tippett, Andre 27, 29, 32
Vinatieri, Adam 38, 39
Welker, Wes 43